D1193770

THE GOOD
THE BAD &
THE TROUBLED

Eduardo M. Arroyo

Published with the valuable support of:

Ana G. Méndez University System
and:
Artefacto
Model Offset Printing
Nagnoi, Inc.
WorldNet Telecommunications, Inc.

Dedication

This publication is dedicated to Don Julio Navarro, retired Executive VP of the legendary Cortés Chocolate Empire, and Dr. Victoria de Jesús, Senior Human Resources Vice President of the over 40,000 students' strong Ana G. Mendez University System, for their valuable and voluntary encouragement that together literally pushed me into sharing this methodology with the world.

Index

Preface 9

Acknowledgements 17

Getting Started 25

The good, the bad and the troubled 48

The Good 58

The "Good" Protocol 71

The Bad 77

The "Bad" Protocol 81

The Troubled 95

The "Troubled" Protocol 98

A note for all the protocols 106

A note on "STOP, START, CONTINUE" 108

Implementation of the Primary Responsibilities Sheet 109

An Experienced Facilitator's
Experience By: Edgar Quiñones 116

A final word from Eduardo
Contending with a Culture of Forgetting 129

Profile: Eduardo M. Arroyo 132

Preface

This book will clarify the path to your success. It will guide you to translate your daily tasks and those of your employees to the achievement of the dreams and aspirations of your business. To begin this process let's get a basic understanding of what you will be reading. The good, the bad and the troubled are employee assessment categories that are defined by an employee's performance related to the objective expectations written in the Primary Responsibilities Sheet. With these three categories, Mr. Arroyo describes with remarkable clarity and brevity the methods to use them to develop your business towards the achievement of the company's vision, and the employees towards maximizing their potential. The key is that the responsibilities that define the categories flow from an unbroken, objective chain through all levels of hierarchy, and through the mission straight to the vision. Each goal, at all levels, is designed to advance the company towards the vision. Finally, what I particularly admire about Mr. Arroyo and his philosophy outlined in these pages is that he never loses sight of the importance of compassion while still emphasizing the need for firm, decisive and timely action focused on attaining results. Underneath it all we are talking about human relationships after all.

Now, if you are anything like me, your company has a vision and a mission but you would have a hard time clearly tying your and your employees' job descriptions and goals to the achievement of them. At WorldNet our vision is to "Transform the business world to one where companies are uncompromisingly living integrity, excellence, caring and teamwork." Yet, our goals, our daily activities and our evaluation process have not been targeted to achieving this. There has been no clear line linking our daily activities to the accomplishment of our vision. Our evaluation system was based primarily on different subjective criteria depending which department or group in which an employee works. We have done the best we can and are very conscientious about living the words of our vision, but have found it a confusing and an insurmountable task as our company has grown to two hundred employees.

Since then we began to work with Mr. Arroyo and have begun implementing the Primary Responsibilities Sheets, together with the method of evaluation that goes with them as outlined in this book. While it is too early in the implementation phase to see the results throughout all levels of the company, some remarkable things have already occurred. First, the overwhelming feeling I had when trying to implement our vision and mission has lifted like fog in the afternoon sun. Second, my energy and passion have increased as my focus has clarified and sharpened. Finally, my anticipation and anxiety have grown, and I can plainly see the dysfunction within my company (although very good as per traditional standards) relative to the extraordinary results that I now see as possible. While this last observation may be frustrating, it is also exciting to see the potential again.

I must point out that Mr. Arroyo's method of using the Primary Responsibilities Sheet and assessments categories for your employees as a living instrument to guide, focus and control your company is not magic, nor is it a quick fix. It is a well-structured model for success, synthesized from years of study and real world experience. If you are serious about achieving extraordinary results, this is a powerful tool to use. It is very simple, but it is not easy. Just as I am, you will have to work hard to see results. But, the journey is much of the fun when the goal is the attainment of your vision! I hope you use this tool as I am...and keep your ears open to hear news about WorldNet's success in transforming the business world.

David L. Bogaty
Founder and CEO
WorldNet Telecommunications, Inc.

Acknowledgements

I'm eternally indebted to all those that pioneered the testing and development of this methodology, specially the leaders of Airport Shoppes and Hotels Corporation and Surfside Hotels Corporation. Among them, I want to thank José Algarín, Dr. José Santana, Mr. Edwin Santana and Mrs. Maricarmen Borges, who pioneered the use of The Good, The Bad and the Troubled, and have kept on helping me push the envelope of its development, with an unparalleled trust in its possibilities.

This venture would not have been possible without the support of my family and close friends. Specific thanks go to my son Manolo and my daughter Frances Marie, for their help in editing the initial versions of the document, and for Monica, Eduardo and Maria Victoria for their continued support.

Special thanks are in order for Geovanny Del Valle and the ARTEFACTO TEAM, for the artwork and editing. My appreciation also goes to Iris Berrios, Néstor Figueroa, Josè Santana, all of those who over the years have created hundreds of Primary Responsibilities Sheets, and to all our Professional Leadership Academy participants for their help. Mega special thanks go to my longtime partner and brother, Edgar Quiñones, for all his support in applying these concepts.

I would also like to share with the readers the stories behind the dedications of the book. First with Don Julio Navarro, an avid reader and world class executive, who after he received specific instructions from the owner and company president of the Cortés chocolate manufacturing conglomerate that he worked for, sat us down at his office 13 years ago. Without exchanging many pleasantries he asked us how old we were, and after our answers (that asserted the fact that he was considerably older than us), asked "What can you teach me if you are so much younger than me?"

That startling start developed into a long term professional relationship during which I had the opportunity to help him reach his lifetime professional goal of running the organization. Strange as life is, the young guy that could not teach him anything had the honor of preparing the execution agreement under which his dream became a reality. Several years later, after having implemented an earlier version of The Good, The Bad and The Troubled, he again sat me down at his office and said "Doctor, you must publish this methodology". Coming from a person who has consistently read several business books a month throughout his career, I felt flabbergasted. The only words that could come out of my mouth were "Thanks, I promise you I will". Now I dream of taking a plane while the ink of the first books out of the press is still wet, and interrupt his peaceful life as a retiree, to present my promise to him as completed.

The other part of this dual dedication was due to the second and final push received to make this happen. It came from Dr. Victoria de Jesús, Senior Human Resources Vice President of the Ana G. Mendez University System. In spite of a long term professional relationship with Dr. de Jesús, she had never heard this presentation from us. I was sitting several chairs down the table from her while my longtime Associate, Edgar Quiñones, explained the methodology as part of a

Leadership Academy held for the senior executives of one of their main universities. Fifteen minutes into the explanation, Dr. de Jesús passed me a napkin with a written message: "You have to copyright and sell this methodology… you are losing money by not doing so!!!!" This was the first time that she has told me anything even close to that, so I had to listen.

So, because of all these people that valued and trusted this work, and pushed us to share it, here we go.

GETTING STARTED

The leaders' work is getting ever increasing results by provoking favorable and sustainable changes in a system. "Results" are the creation of value. Value is something of benefit to someone. At the end, benefit usually becomes a feeling: wellbeing. Value is defined by your mission. Every activity that consumes resources and does not add value as defined by your mission, is a waste and should be eliminated.

Effectiveness is to create more value at a proportionally decreasing cost. Working on cost, although important, is a limited endeavor. Care should be taken to ensure that decreasing cost does not harm your value creation capability. The only limit to creating value is inside your own head. It is limited by your creativity and by your courage to address change. People, organizations, and countries change through one or both of two processes: inspiration and desperation. A leader should be able to lead by and through both but should never artificially or purposefully provoke desperation.

A mission is a statement of why an organization exists in terms of their value-adding proposition. A vision is the conceptualization of a dream about a dramatically better future. That future normally implies reaching a significantly higher value-creating effectiveness than what it is today.

An organizational system is the set of people, processes, equipment, and facilities that are brought together to perform a mission. Leaders work through formal or informal organizational systems. Their ability to transcend and create value is proportional to their ability to integrate efforts in an engaging fashion. Formally, we have defined 5 major responsibilities for a leader: T.E.D.A.S. (or "to give yourself" as spelled in Spanish).

T.E.D.A.S.

1. Talent management (attract, utilize, develop and selectively retain).

2. Expectations that are fair and clear (no surprises).

3. Dialogue to synchronize and engage talent.

4. Accountability for delegated responsibilities.

5. Systems development.

T – Talent Management

A leader's impact and scope is infinitively expanded or greatly limited by the talent he can engage and effectively utilize towards his cause. The first task is attracting. If the working atmosphere and the level of inspiration is attractive for the type of talent that you need, recruitment will be relatively easy. Eventually, talented people will knock at your door without you asking. If the conditions are not there, a huge amount of money will be required to have them even consider joining your team.

Once they are in, you have to utilize them effectively. This book addresses that in a clear, no surprises, objective, and fair fashion. Their effectiveness will be dealt with. Development will be a logical secondary effect from an effective talent management process. It can be addressed so that they are better prepared to fulfill their present and emerging responsibilities, and/or by acquiring the knowledge, skills and living experiences, to be ready for a more challenging position.

The last element of the leading talent responsibility, SELECTIVELY retaining, (and I have added selectively to emphasize that it is retaining only those that are both needed and suitable for the challenges ahead of us) is the one that always provoked a "funeral home silence" from the audiences that I have addressed for years. Why? Because the majority of people have a difficult, usually painful, pending performance-related conversation that has been continually delayed and postponed for a variety of reasons. The peculiar silence is a witness of how my two simple words, "selectively retained", have surfaced a situation where our responsibility for holding those conversations has not been met. After you have finished reading these pages, and implemented this methodology, you will never delay this major responsibility again... and better yet, the process will become a painless labor of responsibility and love!

E – Expectations

E.

Clear expectations are the key to excellence in performance. A vast majority of the executives that I know, regularly and unintentionally, fail to do this. The message is so obvious to them that the millions of cultural, developmental, and experiential variables that enter in the interpretation of a requested, even formally delegated, task are easily and inadvertently ignored. This process will attempt to operationally define expected results in order to minimize (it is almost impossible to completely eliminate) this major overlooking problem.

Hurrying is by far the biggest enemy of doing a quality job in the process of transferring a responsibility. Realize that if time is your most scarce commodity, one minute spent in further clarifying a request will most likely save you an hour, a day, a year, or a lifetime of undesired consequences.

To be fair, WORKLOAD is a major consideration. I have yet to meet one executive that is disciplined in understanding and quantifying the required workload for people performing non-routine/repetitive work. Many times the expectations surpass the physical capacity by a factor of 50% or more. This is unsustainable UNLESS the process is changed in such a fashion that the new capacity requirements fall under what is feasible. This usually takes time and a concerted effort.

If the workload is ridiculously high, and in the extreme case that everything else under this model is in place, one of two things will happen. First, the person can burn out. The person's health and/or family support system fractures, and the executive eventually fails or worse yet, loses friends, family, and health (many times irreversibly). Second, the person starts cutting corners and/or "stretching" the truth. In such a case, trouble is just delayed and situations come back to bite them and the organization with a vengeance. The executive's sense of self-worth suffers throughout the whole process, as the person has been forced not to be truthful by the push and desire to comply, and everyone loses.

When the overloaded person is the leader (and I have seen hundreds of cases, to the extreme that I have made a living out of helping/coaching on those situations) the damage is magnified relentlessly. Troubleshooting this requires not only a workload analysis, but recognizing: which of the executives' activities do not belong to them, what is the underlying pattern, what causes the pattern, what will be done to correct the situation, and how to prevent those unfitting activities from falling back into his lap again. Subsequently, the corrective process requires identifying which vital activities are NOT being done as a result of the present dynamics, what can be done to get them going AND what will be done to guarantee their continuation.

Before we leave the wide subject of leaders' responsibility, for which this relatively simple methodology (**The good, the bad and the troubled,** or GBT)) will address all five of them (TEDAS) from a myriad of highly effective angles, two additional leadership essentials must be addressed: democracy and courage.

An organization IS NOT a democracy. Decisions (even when consulted with a plethora of people) are made by the leader who was clearly assigned the responsibility and authority to make them. Participation from your team members and other stakeholders is extremely important. Listening and thoughtfully considering opinions and possibilities is essential to sound decision-making, but at the end of the day, it is your responsibility so it is YOUR decision.

If your decision contrasts the feedback previously received (and generally in all substantial occasions) it is good practice, whenever confidentiality allows it, to explain the context and logic of your decision so people understand it was not a capricious contradiction to the public opinion. Doing so maximizes the possibility of everyone answering to your call for professionalism in execution. Having the right to be heard and considered comes with the responsibility, once a decision is made, to do whatever possible to make the decision a productive one, regardless if it contradicts all your logic and emotions.

Elevating the execution level of a system, and making decisions to aggressively and judiciously create a new future for your organization, requires courage. In my experience with the thousands of leaders I have addressed on the subject of leadership, none of them, and I repeat and emphasize, NONE OF THEM, have consciously associated leadership with courage. Those types of decisions always come with attached risks, and because of the lack of courage to make them many opportunities are lost. I urge you to privately look at yourself in the mirror and ask yourself which important decisions have been delayed, and if that delay has been caused by a lack of courage. If that is the case, and it will be hard to convince me that it isn't regardless of what you may say, do something about it or change your career.

Expanding on the leaders' workload, decision-making, and courageous execution dynamics will require another book. Contact me by e-mail if those considerations happen to be of your particular need and I will gladly support you in addressing them effectively.

D – Dialogue

D.

Dialogue, a bilateral or multilateral sharing and understanding of ideas, opinions or meaning (logos), is essential for an almost infinite number of benefits. Specifically and specially, knowing more about the experiences, aspirations, desires, talents and ideas of the people that support and execute your aspirations will result in a more robust decision or plan. It will also allow for a better fit between necessary activities and the person assigned to them, who will probably become the best and the happiest selection for its execution.

A. A – Accountability

In the complex and interdependent system that is the norm in today's multifaceted organizations, the failure of one of its components to execute as required will usually escalate in a domino effect of amplified consequences. Therefore the leaders, as their primary responsibility, must ensure that all resources are performing as required and that fair and prompt corrective actions are taken when any of them does not.

S – System

W. Edwards Deming taught us that 6% of undesirable results are caused by the people executing a work system (who) and 94% are caused by the system (how). This is counterintuitive, but it is so true. We have learned from a very early age, probably as a toddler, that when something bad happens the first question to surface is: "Who did it?" That causes a huge problem. We need to break that mental association and create a new one:

BEFORE: *Problem=* REACTION: *Who did it?*

FROM NOW ON: *Problem=* REACTION: *How did it happen?*

If 94% of undesired results are caused by the "how" and not the "who": who is responsible for the how?

Again: If 94% of undesired results are caused by the "how" and not the "who": who is responsible for the how?

The answer is simple: the leaders. They have the power, authority and RESPONSIBILITY to control, manage and improve the system.

A system, formal or informal, is designed and maintained to create value, to accomplish the mission. This is done through people, processes, equipment and facilities. People perform <u>routines</u>, repetitive activities that are formally standardized or "haphazardously" performed, utilizing processes, equipment and facilities.

Projects are major, planned undertakings that include activities, dates, responsibilities and resources. They imply a revolutionary and significant change (or replacement, or elimination) of a process. Projects advance the organization towards the VISION. Evolutionary improvements should also occur, probably in a continuous manner, as part of the daily responsibilities of the people assigned to a process.

Leaders are responsible for the effectiveness of their organization (formally and/or informally, directly and/or indirectly). They are responsible for the organizations adaptability, survival, and growth. They do this with people and through their work.

People perform work through three generic formats. The first two, already stated above, are routines and projects. The third one lays somewhere in between. I call the third ones "hallway assignments": those delegated activities that are not routines, but simple enough that does not require a formal project structure.

The leaders' ability to make an impact in the world (through organization, community, country) is either magnified or limited by how well they can work with and through people. Change requires either inspiration or desperation. Their effectiveness depends on how well they can inspire their followers to work towards creating a better future. Inspiration can create the appropriate mental associations, thoughts and emotions. It will subsequently provoke both the effective actions that create the desired future. Constructive change also depends on how well the leaders can help others thrive and build a better future (think, feel and act) as a positive reaction to desperation.

Both inspiration and thriving through desperation require people that take action to accomplish the desired outcome. This book is about structuring and developing: responsibility, accountability and development of talent. It complements my other books, **Results Oriented Execution** (which focuses mainly on the Leaders responsibility on managing major undertakings at a top level) and **The Making of a Leader** (which focuses on strategy development).

"We are here to make another world.**"**

W. Edwards Deming

THE GOOD
THE BAD &
THE TROUBLED

People at work exist in one of three realms; **good** - those that meet or exceed the minimum expectations in all of their primary responsibilities; **bad** - those that do not comply with the established performance and behavioral requirements; and **troubled** - those who are irresponsible.

Those that do **comply, do so in one of two fashions:**

1. Comply with performance requirements and comply with behavioral requirements. (Quadrant A).

2. Comply with performance requirements in the TOP 10%, and comply with behavioral requirements in the TOP 20%. (Quadrant A^2).

Those that do not **comply, do so in one of three fashions:**

1. Comply with performance requirements but do not comply with behavioral requirements. (Quadrant D)

2. Do not comply with performance requirements and do not comply with behavioral requirements. (Quadrant C)

3. Comply with behavioral requirements but do not comply with performance requirements. (Quadrant B)

I have personally asked thousands of leaders, right after explaining the PERFORMANCE QUADRANTS, if they could immediately place their direct reports in one of the QUADRANTS. Over 99% have said yes.

I followed up with a second question: would ALL your direct reports place themselves in the same QUADRANT as you placed them? Over 99% have said no.

Amazing, yes! Surprising, no!

Their answers were fast and confident.

The question is: why do we have inconsistencies in quadrant placement? The answer lays in one of three options:

1. Supervisor and supervised have a different set of judging criteria.

2. Supervisor and supervised have different data.

3. Supervisor and supervised have BOTH a different set of judging criteria and different data.

Behaviors vs. Responsibilities
Performance management logic – Quadrants

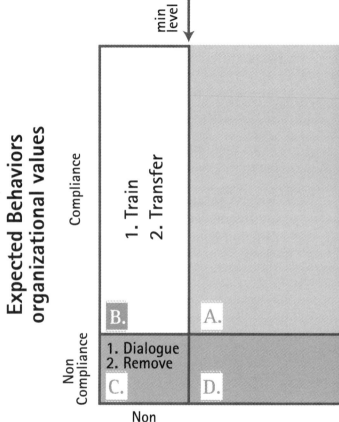

min level

Expected Behaviors organizational values

Compliance

Non Compliance

1. Train
2. Transfer

B.

A.

1. Dialogue
2. Remove

C.

D.

Non Compliance

*models, methods, improvements, opportunities, promotions = retain /
This process is only a suggested guideline. You must verify with your
labor lawyers before implementing

*Top %

1. Develop further
2. Potential for
   more growth

min
level

1. Serious Dialogue
2. Remove relatively fast

Compliance

Job Responsibilities

I have informally asked the following question in over 200 workplaces during the last 20 years:

"How is your evaluation process working?"

I have ALWAYS received one of three answers:

1. We just changed it to a new process that should be better.

2. We are working to change it for a new process that should be better.

3. We are thinking about (need to) changing it.

Amazing, yes! Surprising, no!

Unsynchronized expectations, subjective criteria and different data/results comparison will always create dissatisfaction.

And a last question:

How do your supervisors feel about the evaluation process?

I have ALWAYS received one of three answers:

1. They hate it.

2. I have to follow up continuously. They are not organized, that is why they are always late. (They, usually HRR people, are telling me how they feel, as supervisors of the evaluation process execution).

3. They need training on how to evaluate better; they always give above average ratings to everyone (ditto).

Amazing, yes! Surprising, no!

Out of synch expectations, subjective criteria and different data/results comparison will always create dissatisfaction... AND we procrastinate when we need to do things that are unpleasant.

Therefore, having a process that: establishes and synchronizes clear and fair expectations, establishes objective criteria, and feeds from credible data, will have both supervisor and supervised agree on what performance quadrant the supervised person is, and this will provide the foundation for a workable and agreeable process.

Accomplishing this establishes the foundation for accountability, productivity, growth and development from the appropriate realm: **The good, the bad or the troubled.**

I must explain that I am a student of the late W. Edwards Deming, the father of the Japanese Miracle and of the New Global Economic Order. This implies that I believe, among other things, that individual objectives by themselves segment and limit organizational systems, and they should be inextricably attached to a specific process. Thus the emphasis, as you will soon read, on the agreed-upon changes in the current processes and the execution on those agreed-upon changes as the center of the performance evaluation protocol.

THE GOOD

We define **"good"** as having the appropriate qualities to fit a particular purpose; meeting or exceeding an acceptable standard in performance.

I believe that the good encompasses the majority of workers! You cannot unequivocally know unless "good" is clearly defined. Generically defining "good" covers two areas: execution/results, and behaviors.

In other words, "good" includes what you accomplish as well as how you behave as you accomplish it.

To define "good", we have developed a simple and extremely effective tool called the Primary Responsibilities Sheet (PRS).

The PRS serves many purposes, among which are:

1. Ascertaining how a job/position contributes to the organizational mission.

2. Establishing job responsibilities (a total of between 2 and 7) and how those responsibilities gather the individual's contribution to the organizational mission.

3. Provoking (positively "forcing") a dialogue between a worker (associate, supervised employee, contributor...) and the worker's leader (supervisor) on the subject of the performance indicators that can objectively measure compliance for each responsibility.

4. Defining responsibilities in terms of what measurements (1 to 4 performance indicators) will be used to document evidence of compliance with said responsibilities.

5. Specifying, through those measurements, how performance will be judged.

6. Empowering, through clarity of performance-measurement criteria, the holder of a position to judge his work.

7. Documenting both the dialogue and the final institutional decision on the minimum expected level of performance for each indicator.

8. Giving weight to each performance measurement.

9. Quantitatively and qualitatively scoring actual performance for benchmark and developmental purposes.

10. Instituting a clear, fair, transparent, "no surprises" performance appraisal process.

In addition to these purposes, the PRS is also utilized to help establish criteria for recruitment and placement.

Performance management process

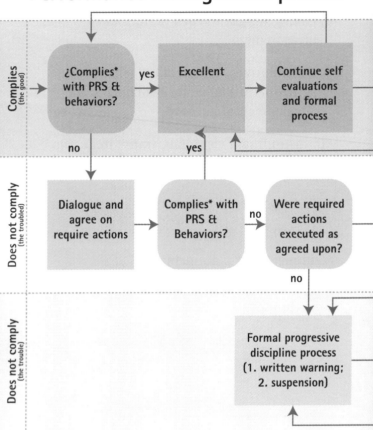

*Major non compliance could result in immediate firing
PRS=Primary Responsibilities Sheet

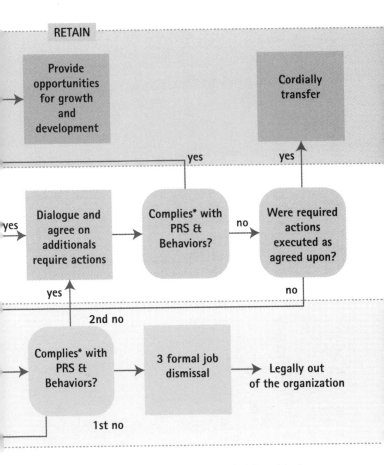

RETAIN

Provide opportunities for growth and development

Cordially transfer

yes

yes

yes → Dialogue and agree on additionals require actions → Complies* with PRS & Behaviors? → no → Were required actions executed as agreed upon?

yes

2nd no

no

Complies* with PRS & Behaviors? → 3 formal job dismissal → Legally out of the organization

1st no

This process is only a suggested guideline. You must verify with your labor lawyers before implementing

Position: President, VP, Director, Manager or Supervisor
Contribution to the Mission: Provide leadership to effectively execute our mission and progress towards our vision.
Revision: Aug 18, 2013

Primary Responsibilities Sheet

1. To acquire, protect, retain, develop and effectively utilize all the human resources and other assets.	Safety : Ensure establishment and Execution of Processes	100% of Policies
	EBITDA or SALES VOLUME	90% of budget
	"Turnover = Involuntary Loss of employees/total emp." anualized.	Decreasing annually.
	Average Percentage of Development Plans of his direct group, measured as Completed VS Projected.	90% of Plan
2. To fulfill the activities required by the Corporate Calendar, programmed formally and executed with the participation of your team.	Percent of activities of the Corporate Calendar completed on time. • Strategic Cycle • Budget Cycle • Commmunications Cycle and other.	90%

3. To ensure fulfillment of the actions scheduled in tha Strategic Plans	Percent of Completed Strategic Actions and/or Emergent Strategic Actions VS Budgeted or Emergent Actions, as negotiated and planed.	90%
4. To fulfill the administrative routines of informing, communicating, revising, developing and improving people and processes.	Percent of Monthly Execution Reports, including Critical Parameters Systems Management, completed VS required, according to formats and on time.	90%
	Formal one on one meetings with his staff.	Monthly
	Quarterly one on one meetings with direct reports to revise the execution of their PRS. (list here critical parameters assigned)	Quarterly
5. To develop and maintain a professional, dynamic, and successful Corporate Image.	Quantity of public activities that will improve our image.	Min 4 per year.
	Behavior as per Corporate Values	Compliance as per his supervisor.

*To receive a free WORD file of a complete blank PRS form please e-mail me at eduardo@e-arroyo.com and write PRS-FORM in the subject line.

The components (heading, footer and columns) of the PRS are:

1. Position (heading)

2. Contribution to the Mission (heading) - A one sentence statement synthesizing the value creation responsibility that merits the creation and sustainability of the position.

3. Document revised date (heading) - Last date when the document contents (not the input of actual performance data) was revised.

4. Performance period (heading) - Period of time covered by performance data.

5. Responsibilities (first column) - The set of top level duties or obligations for which this position is held accountable. Top level implies broad coverage, in such a fashion that any position will be described with between a minimum

of 2 and an absolute maximum of 7 responsibilities. For example, cleaning is not one of the janitor's responsibilities; it is a task or activity. One responsibility of a janitor is safeguarding the hygiene and health of those utilizing a specified infrastructure. The responsibilities must go hand in hand with the stated contribution to the mission.

6. Performance Indicator (second column) - Indicators, between one and four, clearly reflect how well a particular responsibility is executed. Each indicator should be operationally defined. In other words, they should have a defined mathematical formula that clearly shows how the component data that generates the performance number is gathered and manipulated.

7. Performance Expectation Level (third column) – At what minimum acceptable level (MAL) number/requirement an

employee, with the experience and talent of the position holder, is expected to perform for each indicator. As an option, a SET (Superior Expectation Target) could also be established in order to always strive to sustainably increase performance of the process design and execution.

8. Weight - If necessary, we have given different weight to various responsibilities/measurements in some applications, in order to reflect management priorities at the time.

9. SET & MAL Agreement documentation section – Under each stated responsibility, a blank area is left to record significant accomplishments (as compared with SET, Superior Expectation Targets), significant opportunities, or formal agreements established to meet and surpass MAL. Surpassing SET level requires a note

explaining which process design changes where utilized to sustainably achieve this new level. When a scoring system is utilized to benchmark a period's performance, performance below a MAL level could mean a score of ZERO and a score at or above a SET level might imply a multiplier or higher weight.

To institutionalize expected behaviors, all PRS's must include a responsibility addressing the compliance with Corporate Values and employee manual. Your Corporate Values should be expanded and explained so that the anticipated behaviors are as clear, observable and objective as possible.

> **"Remember, Eduardo, there is no substitute for knowledge."**
>
> *W. Edwards Deming*

THE "GOOD" PROTOCOL

The review process is implemented at an absolute minimum of every four months. Some people do it monthly. I recommend starting every other month and then moving to quarterly. The review process is scheduled in the corporate calendar (an annual publication of planned dates for milestones of mayor business cycles such as budgets, strategic planning and execution reviews, organization wide structured communications cycles, performance reviews, development plans cycles and succession planning, among others, which are part of the executives' responsibilities to execute on a timely and complete fashion).

The review is scheduled and executed bottoms up. It starts at the lower organizational levels and builds up to the VP's one-on-one review sessions with the president; and, maybe higher up, to the President and the Board of Directors (or with a special board committee. This may happen annually at this level, but at least twice a year is recommended). There are at least two reasons for this. One, execution evidence/numbers are built up through the levels. Second, a self-checking tool is built in the process, to verify the responsibility of all people that have direct reports to comply with the one-on-one sessions. When each session is executed, the supervisor ensures that the person under review has reviewed the performance of all direct reports.

During the review session, the supervised person presents evidence of compliance (or lack of) for each of the established measurements. This is an extremely important design parameter since it eliminates much of the historical procrastination (passive avoidance) of supervisors towards the performance review process. It eliminates the ever frustrating attempt of supervisors to gather and defend performance measurements/facts for each and every one of the direct reports (an overwhelming if not impossible task!).

After each measurement is presented, one of two things should happen. If they are good, congratulations are in order. If they are not good (do not comply with the established minimum standard), the BAD protocol is executed (next chapter). The "not good" (or bad) operational definition should be previously established. For example a less than 80% compliance with the established minimum execution level for an individual measurement (for example having less than a 72% score in a parameter where a 90% was expected... 80% of 90% is 72%), or a less than 85% total score.

If a good overall standing is established, a short discussion follows on what could be done to improve even further, and notes are taken for follow up and learning.

"In God we trust, all others bring data"

W. Edwards Deming

THE BAD

We define "bad" as below a minimum acceptable level in performance (MAL).

The bad usually encompasses less than half of workers... much less than half, I hope. You cannot know "bad" unless good is clearly defined as established earlier with the PRS. Generically defining bad, as good, also covers two areas: execution/results and behaviors. In other words, bad covers BOTH what you accomplish as well as how you behave as you accomplish it.

There are three main categories of bad:

1. Below minimum acceptable requirements in execution/results.

2. Below minimum acceptable requirements in behaviors.

3. Below minimum acceptable requirements in both execution/results and behaviors.

Once minimum acceptable requirements are clearly established and agreed upon then, and only then, we can hypothesize that people don't comply with clearly and formally documented requirements for one of three reasons:

1. They don't know how.

2. They can't (don't have the talent).

3. They don't want to (don't care).

Identifying, and correcting or eliminating those reasons, becomes the focus of the BAD PROTOCOL under the PRS Review Process.

“Whenever there is fear, you will get wrong figures.”

W. Edwards Deming

THE "BAD" PROTOCOL

The first angle for approaching a BAD STATUS addresses the possibility that the person doesn't know how to perform to an acceptable level. A somewhat Socratic (questions-based) methodology is utilized.

Together, supervisor and supervisee explore the actual methodology that results in a "below minimum expectations" score. The supervisor should let supervisee lead the exposition and the supervisory role should be to take notes of the highlights of what is exposed. A proposed list of possible guiding questions is:

What is the actual routine, process, or methodology followed to execute the particular responsibility?

What areas of the process have the largest relevance in not reaching a level of excellence of the particular measurement under scrutiny?

What specifically can be done to drastically improve those areas of the process? Is there anything we could learn by exploring other people within your organization or in other organizations inside or outside your particular industry? What exactly needs to happen?

What, other than the specific actions identified, should the person learn in order to increase a mastery of execution for this and possibly other responsibilities?

Will this course of action positively and/or perhaps negatively affect the execution of this or other system contributors' performance (optimize or sub optimize the individual's performance or the effectiveness of the organization as a whole)? If so, what can be done to eliminate or minimize the negative impact and/or maximize the benefits of the possible actions explored, so that the cumulative organizational impact is positive? Make sure that as part of the planned actions, people that could be impacted by these changes are brought into the process BEFORE implementing.

Could other members of the organization, possibly people with similar responsibilities, benefit from the results of these explorations?

Once this exploration is performed, an agreement on WHAT the person is committing to do differently (STOP doing, START doing, and CONTINUE doing) has to be reached in order to COMPLY with the PRS; or, in other words, to comply with what the person is

ESSENTIALLY paid to do. If the exploration requires investigating what others are doing to improve the performance, the plan should cover and perform these specifics BEFORE deciding on a particular course of action.

Before the session ends, you should have:

Reviewed the STOP, START, CONTINUE agreements for BAD areas improvements, if any could be identified and agreed upon at this stage.

Ensured the person fully understands how to perform the agreed changes, or execute the additional agreed upon explorations and benchmark visits, and that you will be available for further explanations or support.

Emphasized that complying with the agreements is not optional; it is a fundamental job requirement.

Thanked/congratulated for those areas where performance complied or exceeded requirements.

Identified the next steps, including dates and times for follow up sessions and what should happen in those sessions.

All agreements and next steps must be documented in the SET & MAL agreement documentation section.

A note on BENCHMARK explorations: Do not copy processes or activities. Understand which THEORIES (cause and effect relationships) are working under the specific circumstances found, and then explore the possibility of applying those theories to your particular circumstances before deciding on a course of action. It might even be a good idea to bounce your findings and possible applications with the people hosting the benchmark visits to collect their views.

Once the action plan is in place, you will probably face one of these situations at the next performance review session:

All measurements show compliance.

Measurements still do not show compliance even thou agreed-upon actions were executed as planned.

Measurements still do not show compliance but agreed-upon actions were NOT executed as planned.

Other (different) measurements now do not show compliance.

If all measurements show compliance:

Verify that agreed-upon changes were executed. If not, follow similar protocol as TROUBLED, unless other substitutive actions were taken. You must enforce responsibility. You must not let luck run your organization.

If number one above is a yes: celebrate!

Always identify areas to challenge for further improvement, and document for follow up.

Celebrate more, and ensure that changes that caused improvements can and will hold.

All agreements and next steps established to ensure that the new performance levels are maintained must be documented in the SET & MAL Agreement documentation section.

If measurements still do not show compliance, even though agreed-upon actions were executed as planned, use the Socratic (questions based) methodology.

1. Establish:

a. What is the actual routine, process, or methodology followed to execute?

b. What areas of the process have the largest relevance in not reaching a level of excellence?

c. What specifically can be done to drastically improve those areas of the process? Explore benchmarking options.

d. What exactly needs to happen?

2. Agree on what will the person commit to do differently (STOP, START, CONTINUE) in order to comply with his PRS.

3. If this cycle repeats several times and compliance is not reached, you must consider two possibilities:

a. **Under the current conditions, the minimum acceptable level cannot be reached:** Perform a double check to ensure that the person's workload is feasible. Verify performance of others under similar circumstances, internally and possibly externally. Even sincerely project what your performance level would be if you were executing under those specific circumstances, before considering a change in the minimum acceptable performance level (MAL).

If a change in the MAL is necessary, document why and speculate on what needs to happen (major change in product, investment in equipment -hardware, software, etc. - change the executors hiring profile or other major action) in order to be able to raise the MAL.

b. **The person's talents are not aligned with the talents required to do the job, or the experience level is too far behind what you possibly could manage without dedicating an extraordinarily large amount of time for development:** In such a case understand that: it was a placement error (the decision of placing that person, with those specific talents, education and experiences, in that position), establish sincere and non-threatening conversations for moving the person to a position with better fit; or, if such an option is not available, help him as much as possible to a comfortably prompt transition out of the organization.

Then go back to the placement process utilized for getting a person in that position and explore what could be done differently to improve the possibility of a better fit the next time such a placement is made.

If execution results measurements still do not show compliance and agreed upon actions were NOT executed as planned follow the TROUBLED PROTOCOL on the next section.

If other (different) measurements now do not show compliance, something could have changed, or you might have had luck in the past, or just had a particularly unlucky period that requires making your process a more robust one to be able to handle those variations successfully:

1. Follow steps for "If all measurements show compliance" on those indicators that now do.

2. Follow steps on Socratic Method to reach an agreement for those measurements that do not. Make sure non-compliance is due to a lack of a robust methodology. If not, like when no formal procedures for critical processes exists or if they are randomly followed, clarify and formalize the situation, including specific required actions. Establishing those corrective actions prepares the road to fairly follow the TROUBLED PROTOCOL on the next review session if agreements are not followed.

All agreements and next steps must be documented in the SET & MAL Agreement documentation section.

"There is no knowledge without theory"

W. Edwards Deming

THE TROUBLED

We define "troubled" as owning a situation characterized by difficulties or adversity. This troubled situation is a result of a clear failure in executing established agreements that pretended to systemically correct a performance below a minimum acceptable level (MAL).

If all the PROTOCOLS are followed, the "troubled" should encompasses less than 6% of the population. You cannot identify "TROUBLED" persons unless clear and specific improvement agreements are established during the PRS performance review process, consequences for noncompliance to such agreements are previously known by the person under review, and those processes and consequences are religiously communicated and followed by the direct supervisor. Failure by a supervisor to faithfully execute these performance management PROTOCOLS, engrained and highlighted as part of their primary responsibilities and documented as such in their own PRS, is a fast route towards a TROUBLED status for himself.

"If you can't describe what you are doing as a process, you don't know what you're doing."

W. Edwards Deming

THE "TROUBLED" PROTOCOL

Earning a performance status of **"TROUBLED"** should be of NO SURPRISE for the person and an extremely easy, clear-cut, no doubts decision for his leader. The supervisor's agony in confronting those supervisee nonperformance situations will now be gone forever. If a person is in trouble, it is because he earned it by being irresponsible in executing a clearly established agreement.

Gaining this status and facing the risk of losing his job was clearly his choice.

A session starts with the supervisee presenting evidence of compliance, measurements vs. MAL as agreed and documented on the PRS. After this exposition, the supervisor asks what was done to attempt improving the now recurrent noncompliance. To be the protagonist of this protocol, the person had to fail in executing the previous agreement. If he or she does not bring up that fact, you need to highlight it. If the person brings up an excuse, no matter how drastic or dramatic, and he or she had not communicated the situation to you as it happened or on a reasonably timely fashion, requesting your support to manage the particulars, the person IS STILL IN TROUBLE.

These are PRIMARY RESPONSIBILITIES. This is SERIOUS. IF your heart falls for the supervisee, DON'T let it happen. If you do, you will be putting the health and effectiveness of the organization, and of all its employees and families, in peril. Even if this was NOT the case, doing so will make you impotent as an agent of development, since subconsciously it will affect the trust your supervisee had developed in you. Trust is needed for you to become an agent of viable behavioral changes and improvements (for more on this, see Dr. William Glasser's Reality Therapy). If you do let your heart fall for the supervisee, YOU THEN BECOME THE IRRESPONSIBLE (TROUBLED) ONE.

Your script, to be followed in a low, slow and calm fashion, will be a simple one:

"You failed me. I invested time on helping you comply with the minimum requirements of your position, made an agreement on what you clearly and specifically needed to do to attempt an improvement in your performance, made sure you knew exactly what to do, kept my doors opened for if you needed any type of help in complying with the agreement, and you were extremely clear on the consequences of noncompliance with the agreement... irrespective of all that you failed to comply."

If the supervisee still brings up an excuse, your answer should be:

"You failed me and the organization. If I let this go by without consequences, I will be hurting the organization and I will become the irresponsible one... and I will not be irresponsible"

If he continues without accepting, you stop him.

"End of conversation; you failed me. If you fail me again in the next TWELVE MONTHS, I will interpret that behavior as you not wanting your job. I want that job to be yours, but I cannot do anything if you act as if you do not want it"

If the failure is in a critical area, it might imply firing him on the act. Other circumstances might entail a written warning or suspension. Two, three or X times through this cycle within a specific period could earn him a firing. You MUST consult your labor lawyers on the specific requirements needed to legally manage non-performance and execute a firing of an employee in your particular country and jurisdiction. The process presented here is for illustrative purposes only, and by no means does it pretend to suggest or imply a particular process for you to legally handle non-performance.

Once you are professionally clear on the specific legal process you will follow, the same should be documented, returned back to your labor lawyers for a final blessing and then deployed so that it becomes formally known by all, maybe becoming a part of your employee manual. It should be then referenced and reviewed with the supervisee as part of this protocol.

"It is not necessary to change. Survival is not mandatory."

W. Edwards Deming

A NOTE FOR ALL THE PROTOCOLS

Your position, no matter how high you are in an organization, does not give you the right to attempt against the dignity of a person nor does it allow you to fail to respect an individual, no matter the size of his fault or wrongdoing. Ever. To be clear, this means no correcting or reprimanding anyone in public, meaning that no one can see your faces nor hear your voices nor read your comments (yes this includes your e-mails' cc's and bcc's, your "let me share this with you but don't tell anyone else" moments, your expressions and your lips) for doing this. It also means never using offensive words, cursing, or raising your voice above a "library lobby" level, regardless of the employee's behavior (whether the person shouts, curses or even tries to hit you). The moment you do so, you lose, and lose big, and for a long time.

A NOTE ON STOP, START, CONTINUE

All changes have one or a combination of three components. STOP... what you must not keep on doing, ever. START... what you are not doing but MUST now do, consistently, and CONTINUE... what you have been doing and MUST keep on doing irrespective of what you STOP and START doing. This is a very simple but powerful concept that is essential for establishing, summarizing, and following up on agreed-upon improvements.

IMPLEMENTATION OF THE PRIMARY RESPONSIBILITIES SHEET

I recommend a top down cascading approach. On a pilot area, for example customer service, I like to come down all the way starting from President, to VP, to Director. The other option is cascading down by level, full breadth. A third option could be a combination of both, by level but not on all areas/divisions.

The President starts with defining its own PRS, and negotiates it, if applicable, with the Board of Directors or a subcommittee of such. The President then asks the participating VPs to write down their own. Usually I let them go down this road, but limit the initial exploration to the second column only (contribution to mission, responsibilities, and then measurements).

On a first meeting they start by reconciling the responsibilities. These responsibilities are normally the same as the President's, but with a limited breadth/scope, and with a more specific/stratified set of Critical Parameters. These parameters are operational performance indicators that directly reflect, at a top organizational level, the execution of the mission, at medium and lower levels, the execution and effectiveness of processes (more about this later).

After responsibilities are reconciled, measurements/indicators are agreed upon. Once this happens, TEMPORARY expectation levels and weights are set. I use the word TEMPORARY, since this is a learning/ evolving process that requires running through it during several review cycles to understand and format into a practical and significant configuration. It takes around 18 to 36 months of use for leaders to really understand its power and effectiveness. Ensure that WORKLOAD is considered when establishing requirements.

Once those first two levels are synchronized, at least two things happen. First, both levels start focusing on their responsibilities and tracking their performance, since each person is responsible for evidencing his compliance with the expected performance. This initiates the clearly established self-judgment, execution liberty, and power (empowerment) facilitated by the methodology. Second, reconciliation of responsibilities and delegation of execution specifics continues to the next level.

I recommend staying at the three top organizational levels an ABSOLUTE MINIMUM of 4 months (ideally six to nine months or at least three full review cycles) so people get a chance to really understand and fine-tune the process before involving a relatively massive amount of additional people.

If you are a mid-level manager, you could get this GBT methodology started in many ways. You just need the determination for doing so. You could give a copy of the book to your boss, and/or the company president, and briefly explain your enthusiasm at the moment you hand in the book. An alternate method is writing your own Primary Responsibilities Sheet and asking (or demanding ...) your supervisor for an audience to synchronize and adjust expectations and subsequently ask for audiences for you to establish and direct the follow up protocols. Once this is done you could then start creating the PRS for your direct reports and encouraging your peers to do so. You could do both things: give the books, and start your PRS synchronization process. If you are a real leader, you must have (or get) the courage to take the initiatives needed to change your reality. I am sure you will be better off for it.

"Best efforts are not enough, you have to know what to do."

W. Edwards Deming

AN EXPERIENCED FACILITATOR'S EXPERIENCE

By: Edgar Quiñones

Partner & Senior Management Consultant

Arroyo & Associates

Being able to help hundreds of managers of all levels, from top executives to entry-level supervisors, have been a privilege and an honor. Effectively applying the principles and knowledge found in this book has provided the framework to greatly improve the operational and behavioral performance of leaders in a wide spread of markets.

For more than a decade and a half I have been passionately dedicated to help improve the competitive position of our clients. In doing so, I have coached many managers; from really good ones to really troubled ones.

Upon meeting each and every one of them I have started my interview with three very specific questions.

What results are your bosses paying you to achieve?

How can you objectively know and prove that you are accomplishing the expected results?

What exactly is expected from you?

To my total amazement, hardly anyone can answer them effectively.

The first question is answered properly with the word: **responsibilities (the Primary Responsibilities Sheet)**. The main difficulties here are:

That the majority of people think of responsibilities as tasks

"Responsibilities" have not been clarified as "results" by the supervisor

In the hundreds of seminars I have conducted, specifically regarding performance management, I have asked the audience to mention three responsibilities of a secretary, for which 99% of the time they have answered; Filing, answering the telephone and updating the boss's agenda. In our point of view all of them are tasks. The mayor issue with allowing people to focus on tasks is that it steers them away from RESULTS. The basis for a responsibility is RESULTS. I then proceed to ask what is the secretaries responsibility regarding the task *filing*? Somebody eventually answers: "To assure that all documents (Physical and Digital) are readily available when needed, to promote an effective business operation".

Only when a responsibility is seen and perceived as a result, can an employee fully understand that in most situations various tasks are needed to fulfill the desired result.

For example "To assure that all documents (Physical and Digital) are readily available when needed, to promote an effective business operation" I would need to:

Safeguard the files (locked cabinet) - to avoid someone taking the files without my knowledge

Assign someone to take charge in my absence - to avoid slowing down the process

Have a register to log any file being used by another person or department.

File correctly

File in a timely manner.

Just to mention a few.

As you can see filing is just one task of many. All employees at all levels must completely understand and acknowledge the results / responsibilities that are expected from them. I have yet to meet one manager that had effectively documented either their or their direct reports responsibilities using the powerful principal just explained.

After understanding responsibilities the next step is to achieve **accountability** from all individuals for their performance. We have been taught that our role is to give *constructive criticism* to our direct charges. In our experience traditional subjective-evaluation processes erode the very nature of highly engaged employees – pride and passion. You see, when someone is told that he or she is 6 out of a 10 in cooperation and he or she believes to be a 10, terrible things start to happen. In a specific occasion I was consulting a manager and his cell phone rang 10 minutes to 5:00 PM, I told him to answer and he said it was his alarm and he had set it 10 minutes before exit time. He used to stay until late, but after his evaluation he refused to stay after 5:00 PM because his boss gave him a 7 in cooperation during his annual evaluation. Why? Because she asked him to stay overtime the one day that he couldn't, but he had a lot of overtime which she didn't acknowledge. Instead, she gave *constructive criticism* to be more cooperative. Final and dreadful result: now he leaves earlier than before.

The secret is; good old objective – quantifiable - mathematical **indicators,** that are updated and analyzed by the person accountable. By implementing specific performance indicators, an objective operational self-evaluation process can take place. A key ingredient in this step is pride. Yes, pride. By no means is being evaluated the same as rendering our own performance results. In one situation someone is telling you what you did wrong. In the other, I am telling my supervisor what my results were regarding a responsibility previously clarified and agreed upon, using graphs or charts in order to show performance status. Am I improving? Am I getting worse? Or staying the same? What am I doing to improve?

If managed properly, this performance review process will yield incredible results. You see, what happens is that usually managers are so busy and in many cases fed up, that when an employee underperforms or makes a mistake the manager avoids speaking at all about the subject until one of two things happen: 1. The manager blows up with anger or 2. They wait until an evaluation process. In both cases they lose.

Managing performance is about professional growth. As leaders, our employees must *feel* that we are assisting them to improve, not pinpoint weak spots, which usually ends up as humiliation. I know that there are employees with high self-esteem that may like criticism but believe me, in my experience, they are the fewer.

I usually teach the people I coach three basic indicators: Quantitative - #, Qualitative - %, and Average Time to Complete or Process a Task. Using only these three I have helped save many a job.

Once they have identified adequate indicators, minimum expectations must be defined for each indicator. Even here I have yet to meet one manager that had effectively documented either their or their direct charges' performance expectations. Many have told me that those expectations are common sense, to which I have responded with a question: do you and your employee think in the same way? How about your spouse or son/daughter? If the answer is no, I always reply there is no such thing as common sense. According to Merriam-Webster Online, the word common means; "*shared by all members of a group*". All members of our groups or teams do not share the same thoughts. Maybe they should but they don't, hence there is no such thing as common sense. All minimum performance expectations have to be identified and agreed upon as achievable. Absolutely no one benefits from unreachable goals. Set them too high and neither you nor your direct charges will reach them.

I will conclude by stressing the importance

of learning how to listen with honesty and empathy while dialoging about performance. You must master this skill in order to achieve spectacular results. In hundreds of interviews with managers of all levels, most of the reasons for underperforming had extremely simple solutions, but the supervisor lacked the ability to listen. I have heard comments like; when I had that position five years ago I accomplished the goals. Maybe that is true, but conditions change, and with only one variable different, output is different. I believe I have learned a great deal more by listening than by taking. Master the skill of listening.

Creating a self-evaluation process based on responsibilities (results), indicators and expectations (the **Primary Responsibilities Sheet**) requires effort and time, but if done correctly the payoff is absolutely extraordinary in results, peoples' pride and overall satisfying work environment. I am totally convinced you will achieve great results too – just go for it.

A FINAL WORD FROM EDUARDO – CONTENDING WITH A CULTURE OF FORGETTING

Organizations tend to repeat the same mistakes over time. Individuals tend to, willingly or unwillingly, forget the lessons and agreements of the past. Formal systems like this one provide the means of institutionalizing organizational learning, and serve as a depository of that learning's evaluation. We will all make more mistakes and will have to face many difficult situations, but we will minimize the chances of repeating the same mistakes if we use the tools that can help us prevent them.

Let us take the time to assimilate the lessons learned. Let us make the effort to remember those lessons and let us work on implementing The Good, The Bad, and The Troubled to make our lives easier and more productive, and our organizations more effective. It will take you 18 months to fully understand, implement and master it. Have the courage to have an impact. Be a LEADER. Do it now.

"Learning is not compulsory... neither is survival"

W. Edwards Deming

PROFILE: EDUARDO M. ARROYO

Eduardo M. Arroyo graduated with a Bachelor of Science in Management Engineering, a Minor in Industrial Psychology, and a Masters in Business Administration from Rensselaer Polytechnic Institute in Troy, New York before turning 22 years old. He became one of the youngest General Managers ever to run a high-technology organization, when at the age of 25 he was promoted to that position for Microdata

Corporation. He later held the position of Vice-President and General Manager for Emulex Caribe Inc., which he occupied for 10 years.

In 1992, he opened and still directs his own management consulting firm -- Arroyo & Associates -- specializing in Leadership, Management, Process and Quality Improvement Systems, Teamwork, and Strategic Thinking-Planning, for manufacturing, service, and both local and federal government organizations (over 150 engagements and still counting). He also served as local partner for McKinsey & Company for a landmark educational project.

He has competed successfully in fierce international markets through the application of the latest organizational effectiveness methodologies. While employed, he worked under the direct guidance of internationally recognized consultants of the caliber of Dr. Harold Haller, one of an elite group of Dr. W. Edwards Deming's personal disciples (Dr. Deming was personally aware of this process, and commended its implementation speed – calling it a benchmark), and with Dr. Fred Heslet and Dr. William Osgood, experts in Organizational Development and Management.

He has extensively studied the Deming management philosophy, having helped and learned on four of Dr. Deming's live public seminars. He has also studied the "Theory of Constraints" directly from its creators Dr. Eli Goldrath and Robert Fox; "Human Dynamics" under its developer Dr. Sandra Segal and "Lean Thinking – Learning to See," a treaty on Value Stream Mapping, under its creator John Shook.

Mr. Arroyo is considered by his peers as an authority in Dr. W. Edwards Deming's (father of the Worldwide Quality Movement, and the creator of Japan's Industrial Revolution) philosophy.

He has held leadership positions in boards of directors for several organizations including the Puerto Rico Manufacturers

Association. He is the Past-President and still an active board member of the non-profit organization PR2000, whose mission is to advance the competitiveness of Puerto Rico).

Currently he is a Director and Corporate Secretary for Santana Enterprises Conglomerate (Hotels & Casinos, Food and Beverage, Real State, Airline Catering, Food Processing Plants, and Airport Services for Corporate Jets).

He served for many years as volunteer Corporate Secretary for a Nationally Recognized College Preparatory School in San Juan - Saint John's School.

In 1994 he published a very successful leadership guide titled "The Making of a Leader" (based on Deming's "organization as a system" concept and authorized in writing by Dr. Deming himself). His second book, an extremely successful training manual for teamwork called "Trabajando en Equipo" (Working as a Team), was published in early 1995. "The Making of a Leader" was republished in 2002 as an e-book, which has reached the United States, Canada, Bolivia, Mexico, The Caribbean, Australia, Malaysia, India, the Republic of Macedonia, Jordan and South Africa, among a total of 105 countries.

In September 2007 he published his most recent book* "RESULTS ORIENTED

EXECUTION", published by Arroyo &
Associates International Publishing and co-
published with SUAGM, a major university
system with 40,000 students in several states
(*in Spanish, subsequently published in
English as an e-book in 2008).

He has received many formal and
informal awards and recognitions, including
an Almirante Juan Almézquita Award, the
maximum recognition given by PROCOMP
for his support on developing the Island's
competitiveness. He is listed as part of the
TOP TEN group of management consultants
for Puerto Rico and the Caribbean.

*For more information please visit:

www.arroyoint.com

www.e-arroyo.com

CONTACT INFORMATION

Eduardo M. Arroyo

(787)529-0454

eduardo@e-arroyo.com